# What Is Exercise Science?

Illustrations:      Janet Moneymaker
Design/Editing:  Marjie Bassler

What Is Exercise Science?
ISBN  978-1-953542-02-1

Published by Gravitas Publications Inc.
www.gravitaspublications.com
www.realscience4kids.com

How does my body jump a rope?

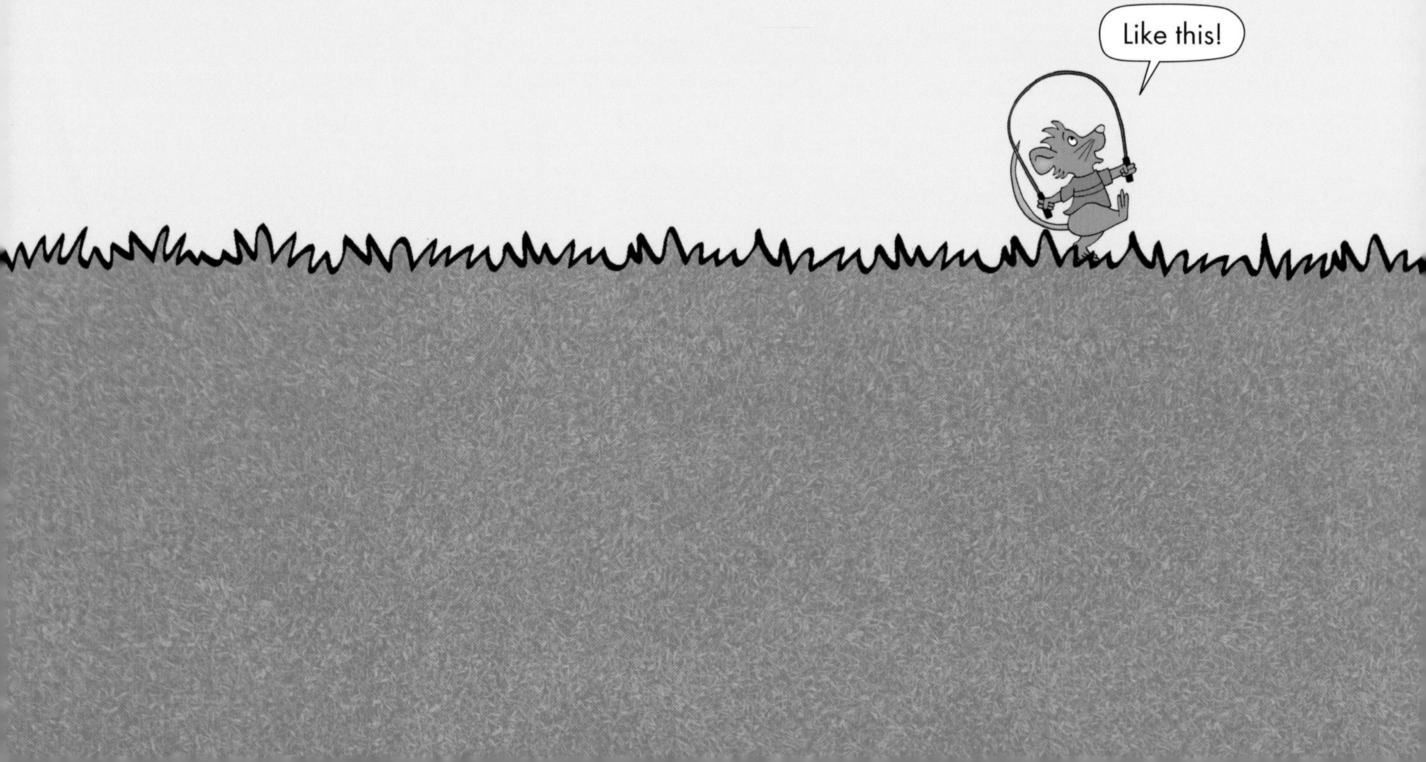

How does my body know

how to climb a tree?

How can I feed my body
so I can lift heavy things?

All of these questions are studied by exercise science.

Exercise science explores...

...how the body works,

...how exercise changes the body,

...how the body uses food.

Exercise scientists

want to find out...

...the best way to feed a swimmer...

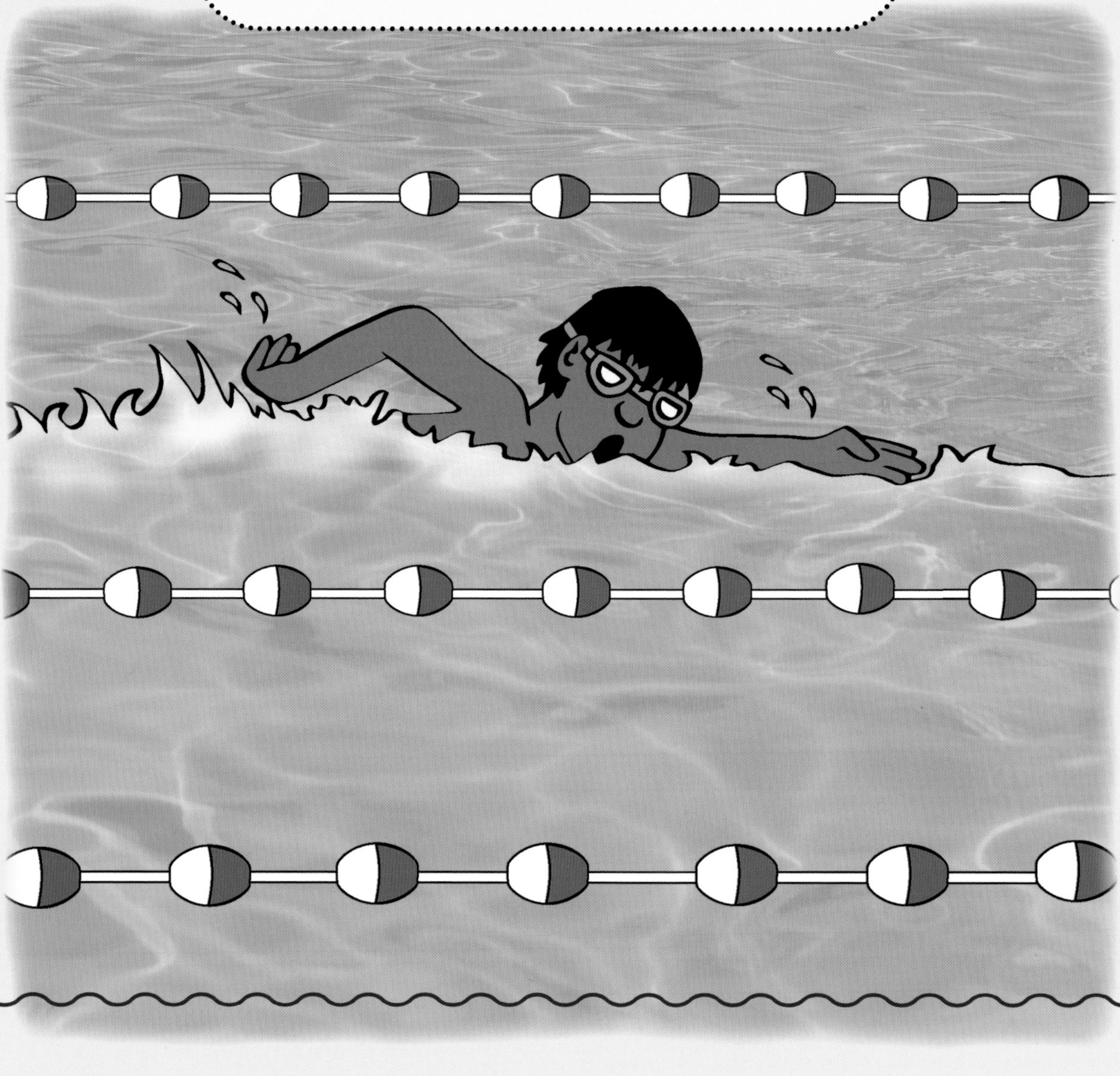

Exercise science

can help us...

## How to say science words

**exercise**   (EK-suhr-siyz)

**healthy**   (HEL-thee)

**muscle**   (MUH-suhl)

**science**   (SIY-ens)

**scientist**   (SIY-en-tist)

# What questions do you have about

# EXERCISE SCIENCE?

# Learn More Real Science!

## Complete science curricula from Real Science-4-Kids

## Focus On Series

**Unit study** for elementary and middle school levels

**Chemistry**
**Biology**
**Physics**
**Geology**
**Astronomy**

## Exploring Science Series

**Graded series** for levels K–8. Each book contains 4 chapters of:

**Chemistry**
**Biology**
**Physics**
**Geology**
**Astronomy**